Count It

DOVER PUBLICATIONS,
MINEOLA, NEW YORK

Bibliographical Note

Count It, first published by Dover Publications, Inc., Mineola, New York, in 2015, contains all of the pages from the following online workbooks published by Education.com: *Awesome Addition, Dive Into Data, Navigating Numbers, Patterns on the Go,* and *Word Problems, No Problem.*

International Standard Book Number

ISBN-13: 978-0-486-80260-2
ISBN-10: 0-486-80260-4

Manufactured in the United States by Courier Corporation
80260401   2015
www.doverpublications.com

CONTENTS

AWESOME ADDITION

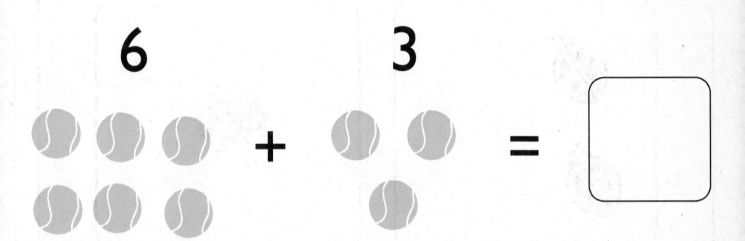

6 + 3 =

DRAW TO ADD

*Follow the directions and add more objects.
Then count them up to answer the questions!*

Draw 2 more ladybugs.

*Now there are
____ ladybugs!*

Draw 4 more leaves.

*Now there are
____ leaves!*

Draw 5 more coconuts.

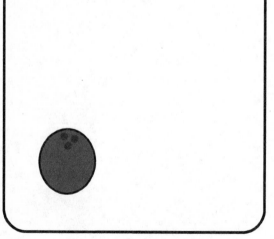

*Now there are
____ coconuts!*

Draw 1 more apple.

*Now there are
____ apples!*

Circus Math

How many of each picture do you see? Add them up and write the number in the box!

1 + 1 =

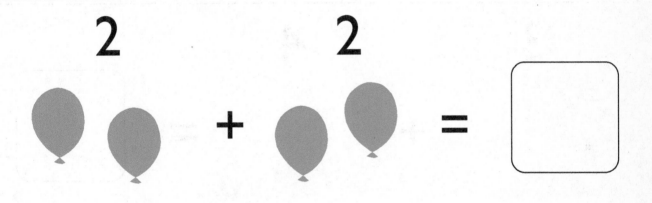

2 + 2 =

2 + 1 =

3

Bath Time Math

How many of each picture do you see? Add them up and write the number in the box!

4   1

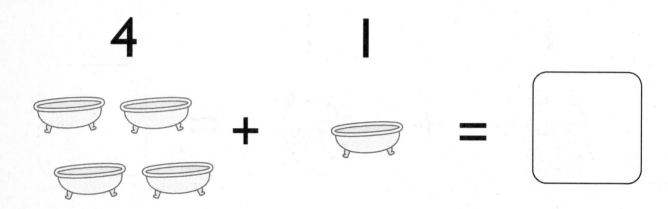

3   4

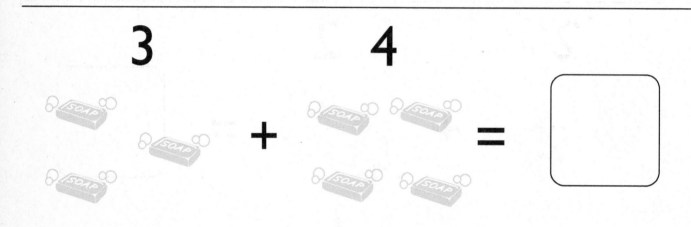

4   2

4

easy

Sports Math

How many of each picture do you see? Add them up and write the number in the box!

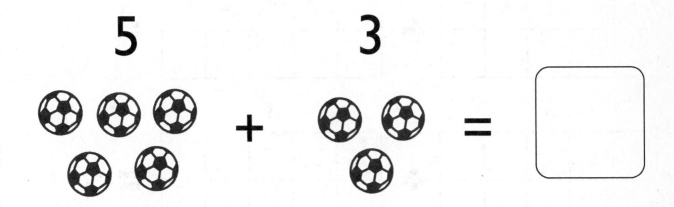

5 + 3 =

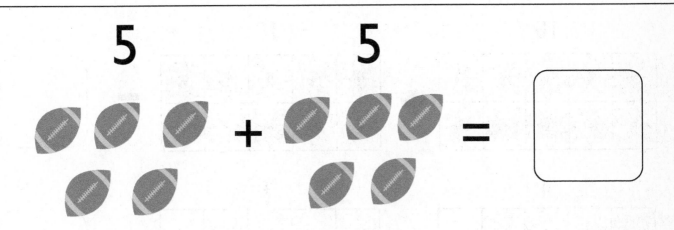

5 + 5 =

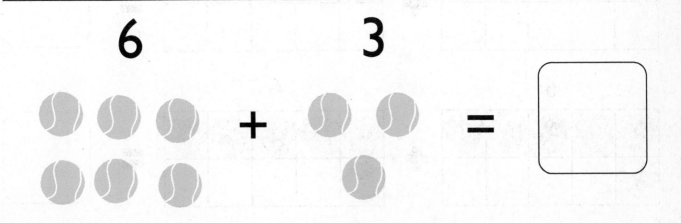

6 + 3 =

Adding Spring FLOWERS!

How many do you see? Add them together!

5 + 5 = ☐

3 + 3 = ☐

10 + 10 = ☐

4 + 4 = ☐

6 + 6 = ☐

What pretty FISH!

How many pictures do you see? Add them up.

Adding Under the Sea!

Add together the sea animals in each box, then write
your answer in the box on the right.

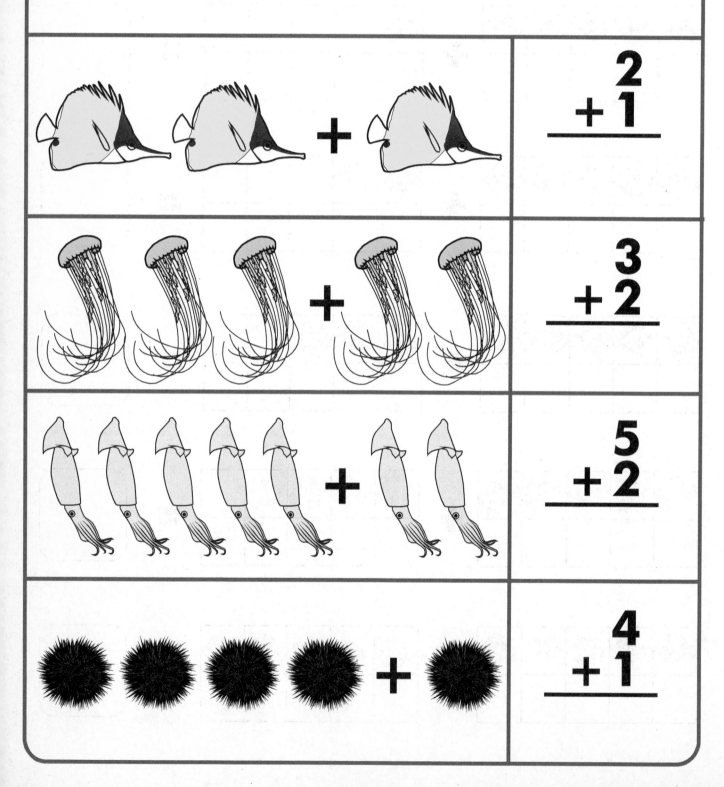

$$\begin{array}{r} 2 \\ +\,1 \\ \hline \end{array}$$

$$\begin{array}{r} 3 \\ +\,2 \\ \hline \end{array}$$

$$\begin{array}{r} 5 \\ +\,2 \\ \hline \end{array}$$

$$\begin{array}{r} 4 \\ +\,1 \\ \hline \end{array}$$

8

Instruments
Addition ➕

Add together the instruments that are in each box and write your answer in the box on the right.

1

$$\begin{array}{r} 5 \\ +3 \\ \hline \end{array}$$

2

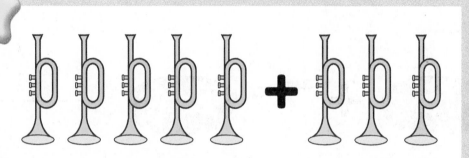

$$\begin{array}{r} 2 \\ +1 \\ \hline \end{array}$$

3

$$\begin{array}{r} 3 \\ +4 \\ \hline \end{array}$$

4

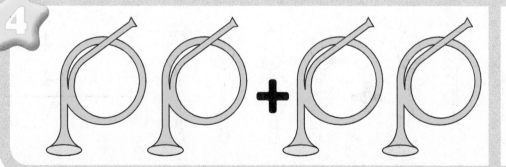

$$\begin{array}{r} 2 \\ +2 \\ \hline \end{array}$$

Kitchen
Addition

Add together the kitchen items that are in each box and write your answer in the box on the right.

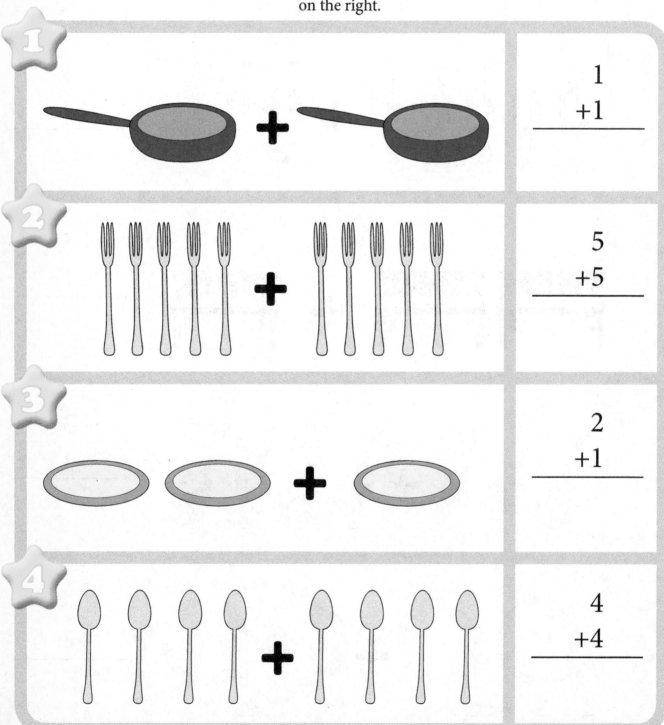

1

$$\begin{array}{r} 1 \\ +1 \\ \hline \end{array}$$

2

$$\begin{array}{r} 5 \\ +5 \\ \hline \end{array}$$

3

$$\begin{array}{r} 2 \\ +1 \\ \hline \end{array}$$

4

$$\begin{array}{r} 4 \\ +4 \\ \hline \end{array}$$

It's Fall!
Addition +

Add together the fall items that are in each box and write your answer in the box on the right.

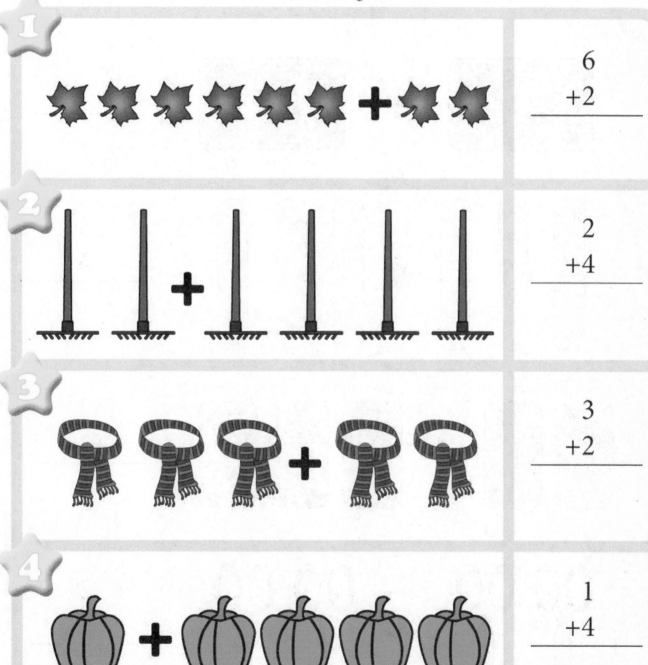

1.
$$\begin{array}{r} 6 \\ +2 \\ \hline \end{array}$$

2.
$$\begin{array}{r} 2 \\ +4 \\ \hline \end{array}$$

3.
$$\begin{array}{r} 3 \\ +2 \\ \hline \end{array}$$

4.
$$\begin{array}{r} 1 \\ +4 \\ \hline \end{array}$$

Back to School

Addition

Add together the school supplies that are in each box and write your answer in the box on the right.

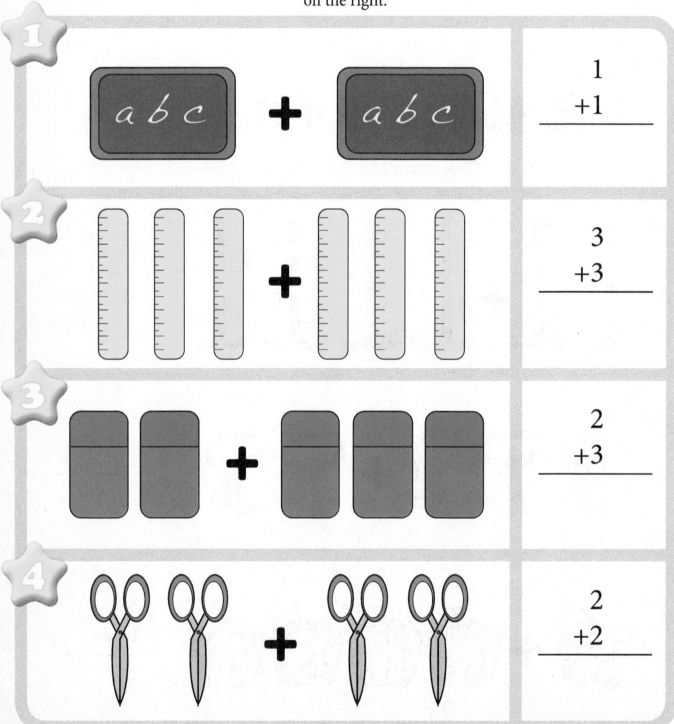

It's Winter!
Addition ✚

Add together the winter items that are in each box and write your answer in the box on the right.

1

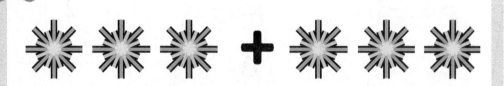

$$\begin{array}{r} 3 \\ +3 \\ \hline \end{array}$$

2

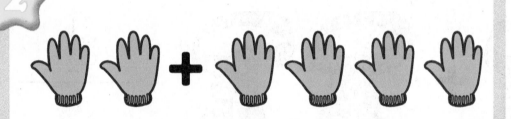

$$\begin{array}{r} 2 \\ +4 \\ \hline \end{array}$$

3

$$\begin{array}{r} 1 \\ +2 \\ \hline \end{array}$$

4

$$\begin{array}{r} 4 \\ +1 \\ \hline \end{array}$$

Wear It!

Addition +

Add together the clothes that are in each box and write your answer in the box on the right.

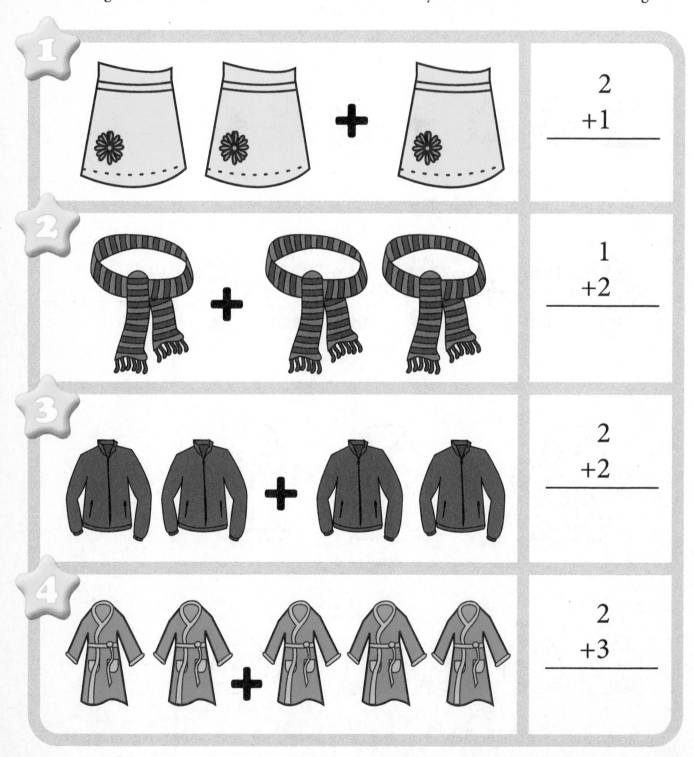

1.
$$\begin{array}{r} 2 \\ +1 \\ \hline \end{array}$$

2.
$$\begin{array}{r} 1 \\ +2 \\ \hline \end{array}$$

3.
$$\begin{array}{r} 2 \\ +2 \\ \hline \end{array}$$

4.
$$\begin{array}{r} 2 \\ +3 \\ \hline \end{array}$$

Tools
Addition

Add together the tools that are in each box and write your answer in the box on the right.

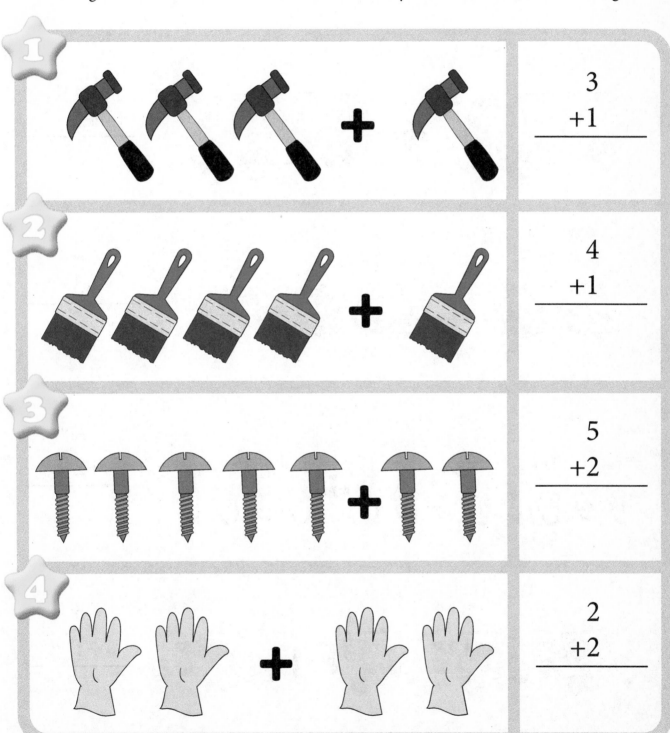

1. 3
    +1
    ___

2. 4
    +1
    ___

3. 5
    +2
    ___

4. 2
    +2
    ___

Let's Go!
Addition

Add together the vehicles that are in each box and write your answer in the box on the right.

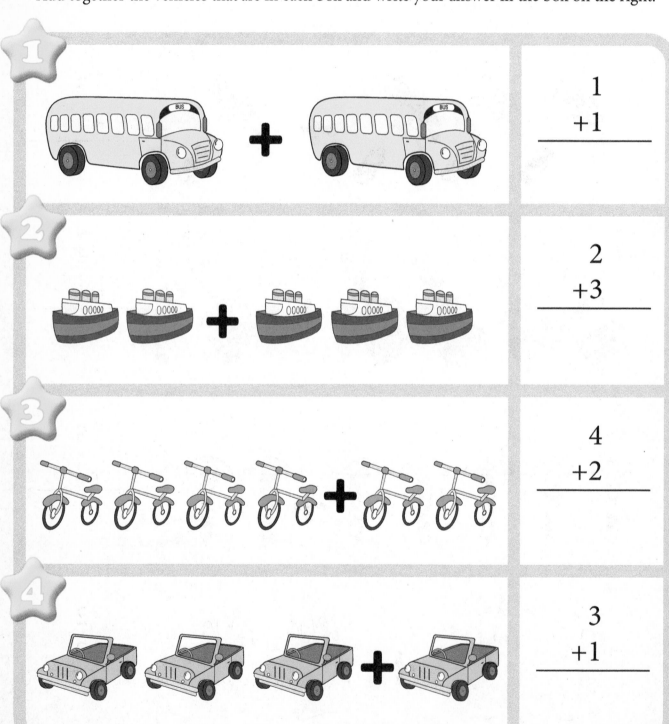

1. 1 +1

2. 2 +3

3. 4 +2

4. 3 +1

ADD THE NUMBERS

Spiky needs help finding the right bone. Add the numbers in each box and color the bone with the correct answer.

2 + 5 = _____
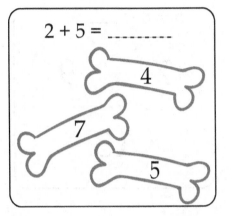

1 + 2 = _____
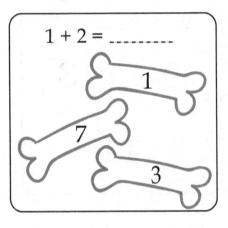

3 + 6 = _____
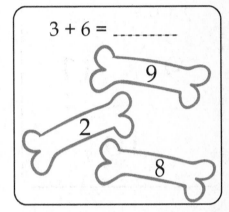

5 + 3 = _____
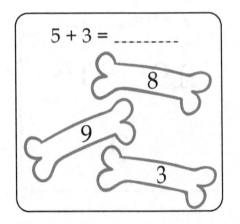

7 + 1 = _____
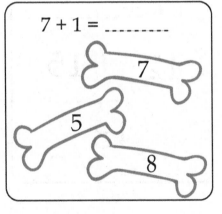

1 + 4 = _____
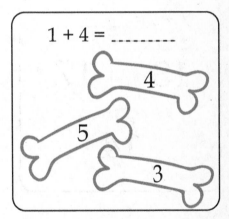

2 + 5 = _____
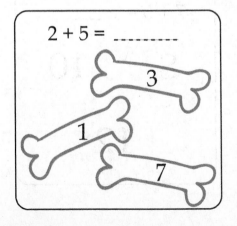

4 + 4 = _____
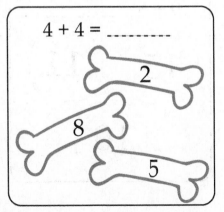

3 + 3 = _____
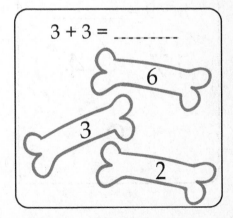

ADD THE NUMBERS

Roger needs help finding the right cookie. Add the numbers in each box and color the cookie with the correct answer.

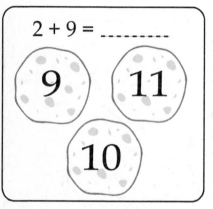

2 + 9 = _____

9   11

10

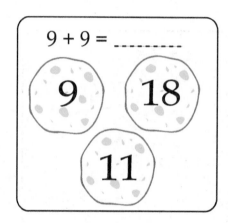

9 + 9 = _____

9   18

11

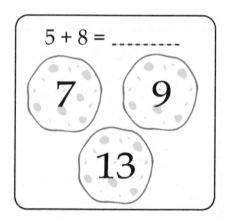

5 + 8 = _____

7   9

13

7 + 7 = _____

13   17

14

8 + 4 = _____

12   15

18

7 + 9 = _____

19   16

9

8 + 9 = _____

17   4

9

9 + 6 = _____

15   11

10

7 + 5 = _____

8   10

12

ADD THE NUMBERS

Ricky the Caterpillar needs help finding the right apple. Add the numbers in each box and color the apple with the correct answer.

2 + 2 = ...

6   4

9

5 + 5 = ...

10   14

11

3 + 3 = ...

3   8

6

7 + 7 = ...

11   14

12

1 + 1 = ...

3   4

2

9 + 9 = ...

13   18

16

4 + 4 = ...

6   9

8

8 + 8 = ...

16   14

18

6 + 6 = ...

11   12

10

ADD THE NUMBERS

Jane needs help finding the right egg. Add the numbers in each box and color the egg with the correct answer.

1 + 7 = ...
19   14
8

4 + 7 = ...
11   12
4
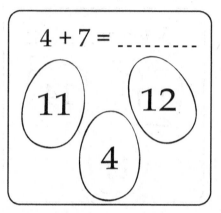

2 + 5 = ...
3   7
17
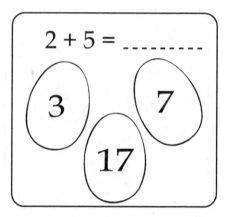

6 + 3 = ...
9   7
10
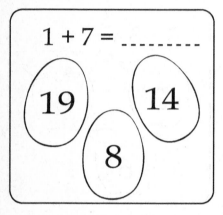

1 + 2 = ...
5   3
4
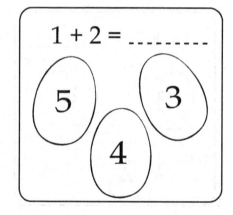

5 + 8 = ...
13   14
9
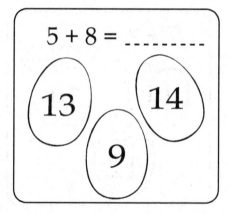

3 + 3 = ...
8   4
6

8 + 7 = ...
10   15
19
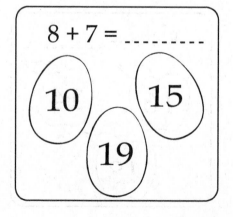

4 + 2 = ...
11   7
6
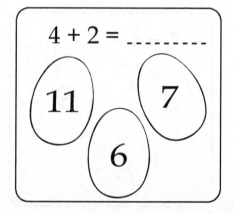

20

Great job!

_____
is an Education.com math superstar

DIVE INTO DATA

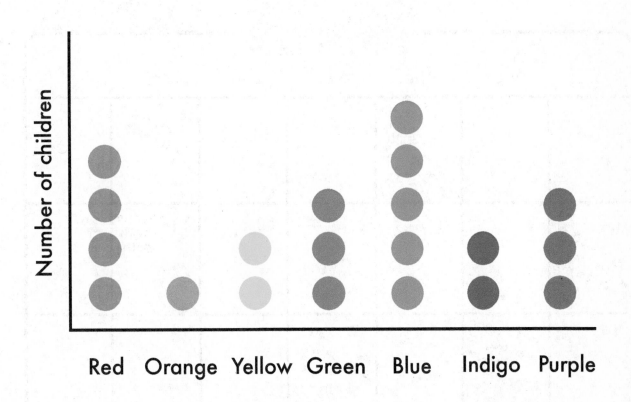

Joey's Calendar

Look at the calendar below, and then answer the questions on the next page.

July

Sun.	Mon.	Tue.	Wed.	Thu.	Fri.	Sat.
		1 Meet up with Sally	2	3	4 Fireworks in the park	5
6 Rock concert at 2 p.m.	7	8	9	10	11 Meet up with Sally	12
13	14 Deliver newspapers at 5 a.m. News	15	16 Call Aunt Lily	17	18	19
20	21	22	23	24 Deliver newspapers at 5 a.m. News	25	26
27	28 Go to the science museum	29	30	31		

Joey's Calendar

1. On what day will Joey go to the concert?

_____

- -

_____

2. How many days after the concert will Joey talk to Aunt Lily?

_____

- -

_____

3. On what days will Joey wake up before 5 a.m. to deliver the newspaper?

_____

- -

_____

4. What will Joey do on the last Monday of the month?

_____

- -

_____

5. On which two days will Joey meet up with Sally?

_____

- -

_____

April Weather

Look at the calendar below, then answer the questions on the next page.

April

Sun.	Mon.	Tue.	Wed.	Thu.	Fri.	Sat.
		1	2	3	4	5
6	7	8	9 *Indoor Recess*	10	11	12
13	14	15	16	17	18	19
20	21	22	23	24	25	26
27	28	29	30 *Power out*			

April Weather

1. On which day of the month was it sunny?

_____

- -

_____

2. On which weekend days did it rain during the month of April?

_____

- -

_____

3. On which day in April was there a thunderstorm?

_____

- -

_____

4. When did school cancel outdoor recess because of rain?

_____

- -

_____

5. When did the power go out because of bad weather?

_____

- -

_____

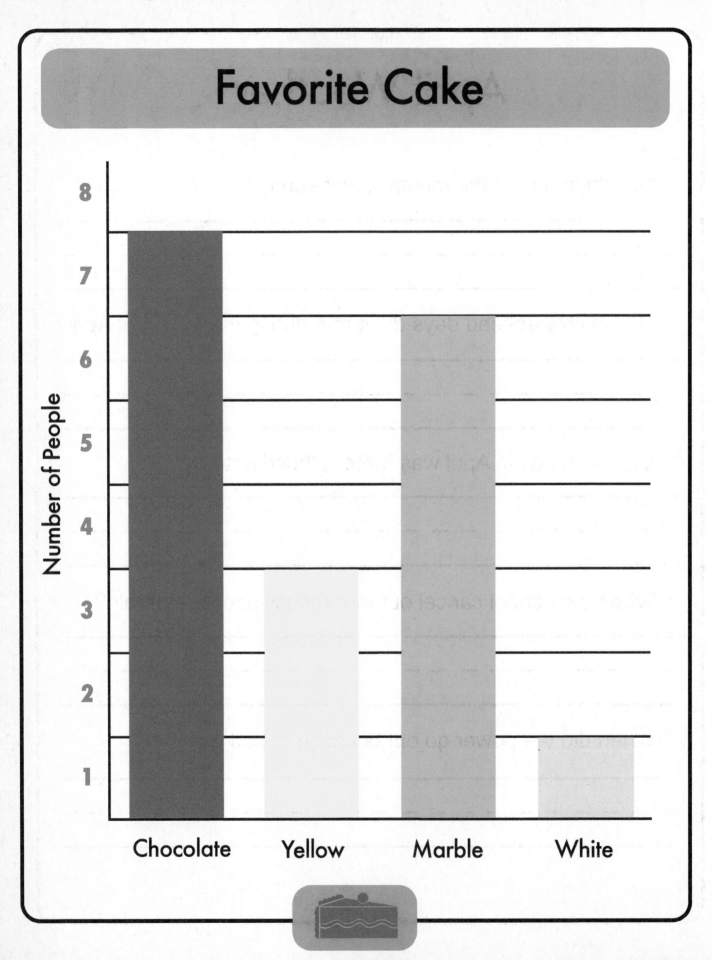

Favorite Cake

Number of People

8
7
6
5
4
3
2
1

Chocolate   Yellow   Marble   White

28

Favorite Cake

1. How many people like chocolate cake?

2. How many people like marble cake?

3. How many people like yellow cake?

4. How many people like white cake?

5. What is the least popular cake?

6. What is the most popular cake?

Robbie Rabbit's Garden Graph

Help Mr. Rabbit count his vegetables by creating a bar graph. Color in the correct number of boxes for each vegetable. The first vegetable has been done for you.

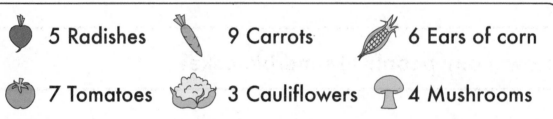

5 Radishes   9 Carrots   6 Ears of corn

7 Tomatoes   3 Cauliflowers   4 Mushrooms

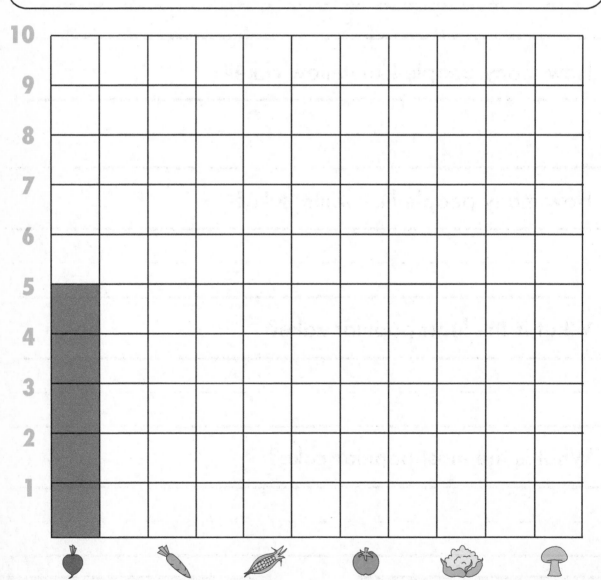

Favorite Colors

Use the bar graph below to fill in your own data! Ask your friends and family to tell you what their favorite color is from the choices below.

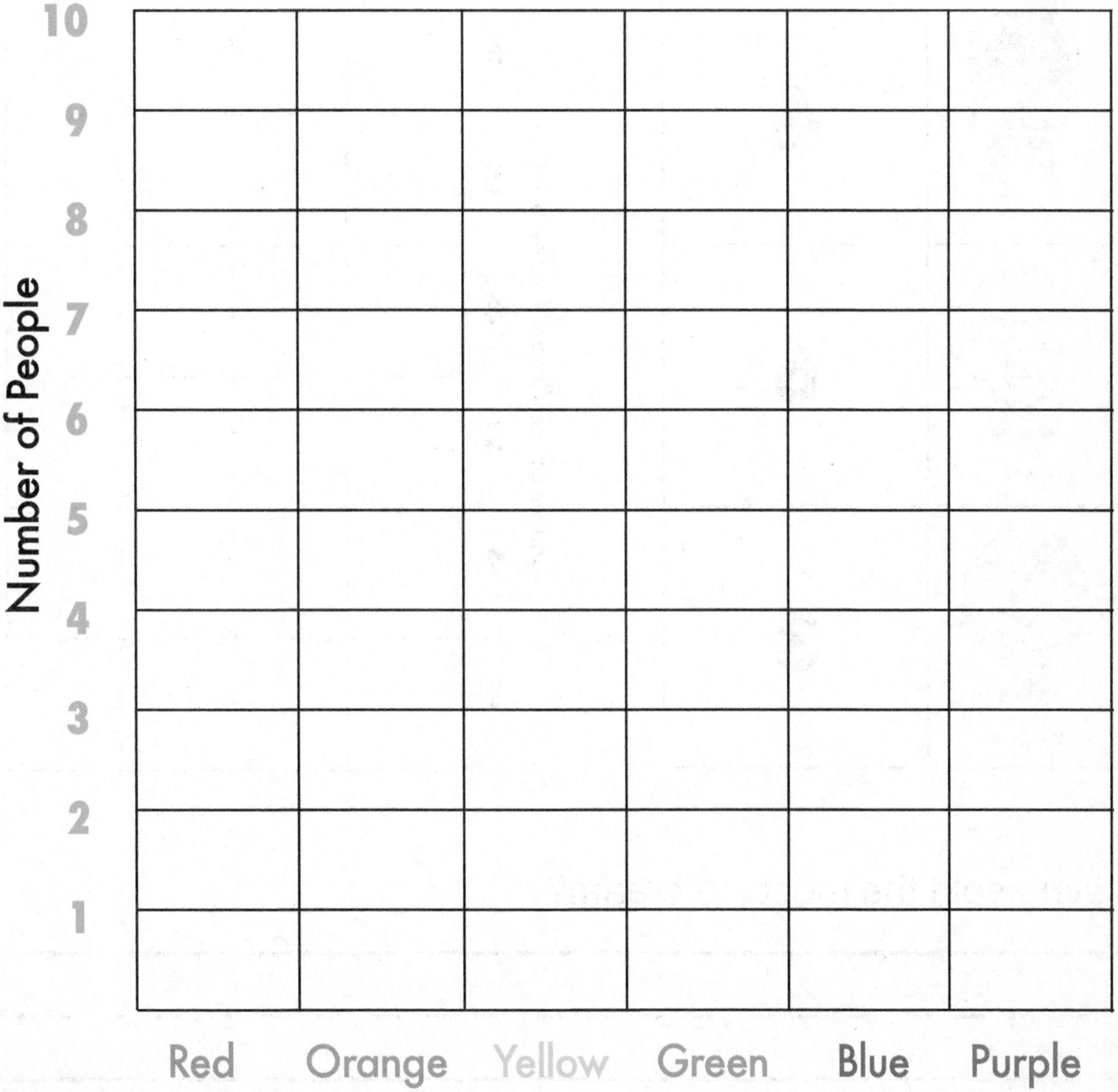

Number of People	Red	Orange	Yellow	Green	Blue	Purple
10						
9						
8						
7						
6						
5						
4						
3						
2						
1						

Ice Cream for Sale!

Use the chart below to color in the graph showing each child's ice cream cone sales. Use blue for Sam, purple for Kate, and green for Becky.

Number of Ice
Cream Cones Sold

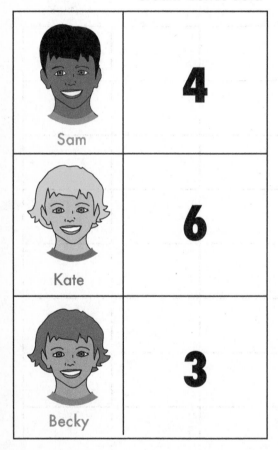

Sam	**4**
Kate	**6**
Becky	**3**

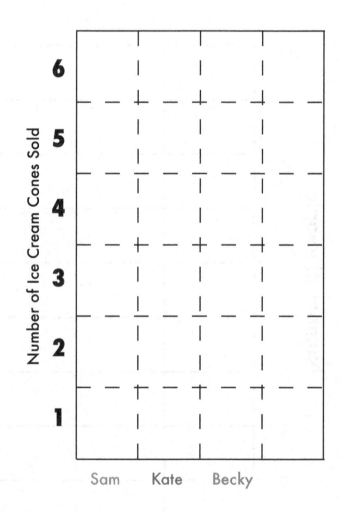

1. Who sold the most ice cream?

_____

- -

_____

Ice Cream for Sale!

2. Who sold the least ice cream?

_____

- - - - - - - - - - - - - - - - -

_____

3. How many more ice cream cones did Kate sell than Becky?

_____

- - - - - - - - - - - - - - - - -

_____

4. How many ice cream cones were sold in all?

_____

- - - - - - - - - - - - - - - - -

_____

5. Sam's friend Jason sold one more ice cream cone than Sam. How many ice cream cones did Jason sell?

_____

- - - - - - - - - - - - - - - - -

_____

Now use a new color to add Jason's data to the graph above. Don't forget to label Jason's data by adding his name under the graph.

Understanding Graphs

Not every graph looks the same. A teacher asked her students to vote for their favorite colors, and she used circles instead of bars to show how many votes each color got.

Answer the questions below to show that you understand this graph.

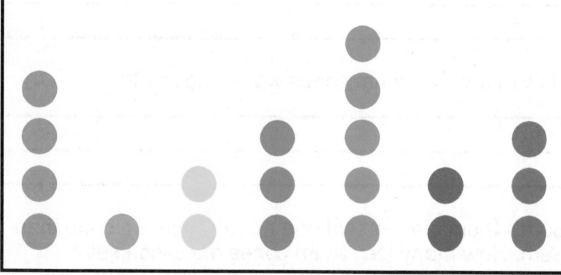

1. How many students answered "green"?

_____

- -

_____

Understanding Graphs

2. How many students answered "red"?

_____

- -

_____

3. Which colors received only two votes?

_____

- -

_____

4. Which color received the least amount of votes?

_____

- -

_____

5. How many students voted for red, orange, and yellow altogether?

_____

- -

_____

6. How many students are in the class?

_____

- -

_____

7. If the teacher decides to use the top two favorite colors to decorate the classroom, which two colors would she use?

_____

- -

_____

The Pet Store

Look at the pictures from Ashley's Pet Store. Count and record the numbers of each pet in the tally chart below. Then answer the questions on the next page.

Type of animal	Tally	Total
Insects	||||	4
Fish		
Birds		
Cats		
Dogs		
	Grand Total	

The Pet Store

1. How many more fish than dogs?

2. How many more insects than birds?

3. Which two types of animals total the same number?

4. Which type of animal is there most of at the pet store?

5. Which type of animal is there fewest of at the pet store?

6. How many pet store animals are there altogether?

Color and Count the Shapes

1. Color all the circles red.
2. Color all the squares blue.
3. Color all the stars green.
4. Color all the triangles purple.
5. Color all the rectangles orange.

Color and Count the Shapes

Count and chart how many shapes there are using tallies.

Shape		Tally	Number
☆	Star		
○	Circle		
▷	Triangle		
☐	Square		
▭	Rectangle		

1. How many more circles than stars?

_____

- -

_____

2. How many more triangles than rectangles?

_____

- -

_____

3. How many fewer squares than triangles?

_____

- -

_____

4. How many shapes altogether?

_____

- -

_____

Minnie's Farm Visit

Minnie visited her grandfather's farm and saw lots of different farm animals. Can you help her record what she found? Use the chart on the next page to organize your data. Record the farm animal totals using tally marks. The first farm animal has been done for you.

Minnie's Farm Visit

	Sheep	~~IIII~~ I
	Cows	
	Ducks	
	Hens	

	Geese	
	Pigs	
	Horses	

Now it is time to count your tallies! Answer the questions below using a number.

1. How many cows?

_____

2. How many chickens?

_____

3. How many more pigs than horses?

_____

4. How many birds altogether?

_____

5. Which two farm animals have the same totals?

_____

Farmer's Market

Help the farmer record how many vegetables he grew in the table below. First count how many of each type of vegetable he has and mark it in the table. Then write it in number form. Finally, answer the questions.

Type of vegetable	Tally marks	Number
Cabbage		
Tomato		
Bell pepper		
Onion		

1. What vegetable does the farmer have the fewest of?

_____

2. What vegetables does he have the most of?

_____

3. How many vegetables does the farmer have in total?

_____

Great job!

is an Education.com math superstar

NAVIGATING NUMBERS

1 2   5   7 8

      14 15   17   19 20

21   23   26   28 29

   32 33 34   36 37

41 42   45   47 48   50

Missing Numbers

Fill in the missing numbers in the chart.

1		3	4	5	6		8	9	10
11		13	14		16	17	18		20
21	22		24	25	26		28	29	30
31	32	33	34	35	36	37	38	39	
	42		44		46	47	48	49	50
51	52	53	54	55	56	57		59	60
61		63		65		67	68	69	
71	72		74	75	76		78	79	80
	82	83	84		86	87	88	89	90
91	92		94	95		97	98		100

Busy Bee

Help Benny the Bee fill in the missing numbers in his honeycomb.

1		3	4	5			8	9	
	12		14			17	18		20
21	22			25	26		28		
		33	34		36			39	40
41		43				47	48		
51				55	56		58	59	
	62	63		65				69	70
	72		74			77	78	79	
81		83		85	86			89	
91				95		97	98		

Egg-tastic

Fill in the missing numbers.

1 2 ___ ___ 5 ___ 7 8 ___ ___

___ ___ ___ 14 15 ___ 17 ___ 19 20

21 ___ 23 ___ ___ 26 ___ 28 29 ___

___ 32 33 34 ___ ___ 36 37 ___ ___

41 42 ___ ___ 45 ___ 47 48 ___ 50

51 ___ 53 ___ 55 56 ___ 58 ___ ___

___ ___ 63 64 ___ ___ 67 68 69 70

71 72 ___ ___ 75 ___ 77 ___ 79 80

___ ___ 83 84 85 86 ___ 88 89 ___

91 ___ 93 ___ 95 ___ ___ 98 ___ ___

Counting from 50 to 100

Charlie accidentally spilled his bucket of tennis balls all over the court. He's already picked up the first 50. Can you help him pick up the rest of his tennis balls by counting the balls left on the court?

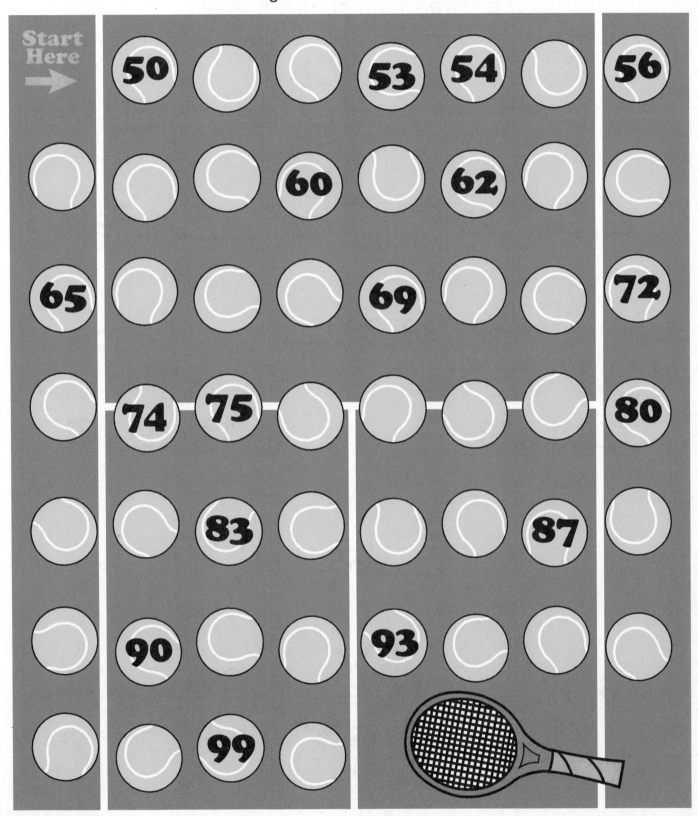

Start Here →

50 · · 53 54 · 56

· · · 60 · 62 · ·

65 · · · 69 · · 72

· 74 75 · · · · 80

· · 83 · · · 87 ·

· 90 · · 93 · · ·

· · 99 ·

Before, After and Between

Fill in the missing numbers that come before, after
or between the numbers shown.

23, ___ , 25   ___ , 60, 61

38, 39, ___

___ , 12, 13   19, ___ , 21

___ , 55, ___

46, 47, ___   89, ___ , 91

Count by Twos

Fill in the missing numbers on the bubbles.

2   4   6   ___

___   ___   ___   16

___   ___   ___   ___

___   ___   ___   32

If there were three more bubbles, what number would be on the last bubble?

___

Hippity Hop

Help Freddy the Frog fill in the missing numbers on the lily pads.

1		3		5		7		9	
11		13		15		17		19	
21		23		25		27		29	
31		33		35		37		39	
41		43		45		47		49	
51		53		55		57		59	
61		63		65		67		69	
71		73		75		77		79	
81		83		85		87		89	
91		93		95		97		99	

Count by Fives

Fill in the missing numbers on the shells.

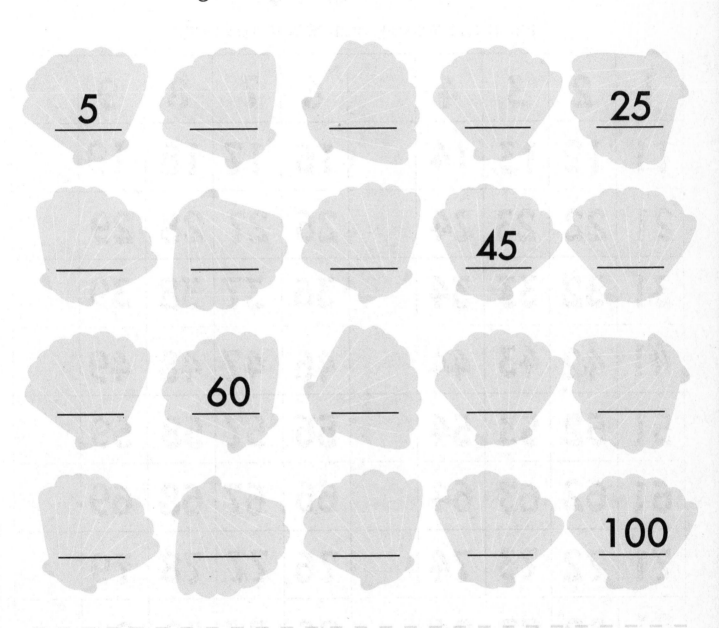

5 ____ ____ ____ 25

____ ____ ____ 45 ____

____ 60 ____ ____ ____

____ ____ ____ ____ 100

If there were three more shells, what number would be on the last shell?

____

Missing Numbers
Counting by 5's

Fill in the missing numbers in the chart.

1	2	3	4		6	7	8	9	
11	12	13	14		16	17	18	19	
21	22	23	24		26	27	28	29	
31	32	33	34		36	37	38	39	
41	42	43	44		46	47	48	49	
51	52	53	54		56	57	58	59	
61	62	63	64		66	67	68	69	
71	72	73	74		76	77	78	79	
81	82	83	84		86	87	88	89	
91	92	93	94		96	97	98	99	

Skip Count by Ten

Each pile has ten candies in it. Count by tens and write the total in the box.

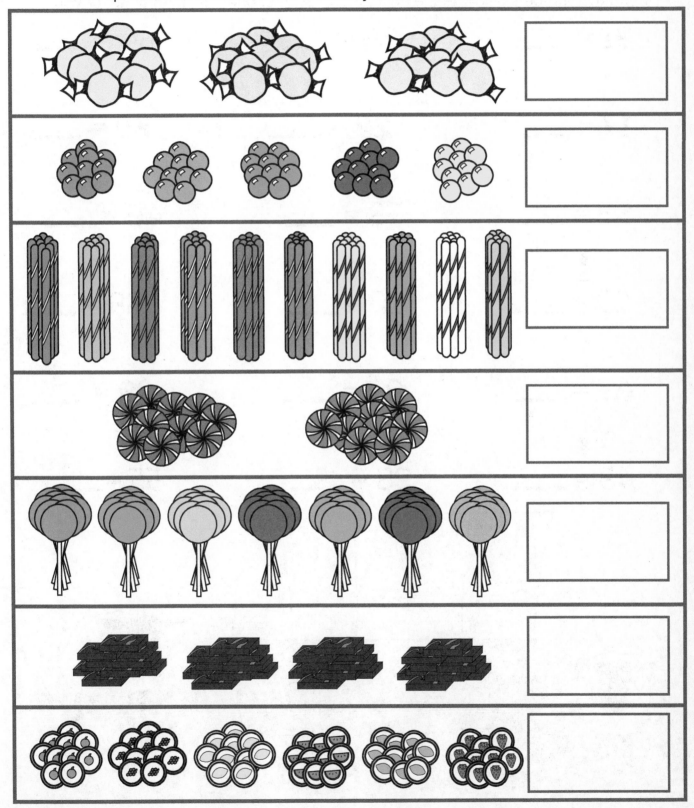

Rounding to 10

Round the numbers below to the nearest 10. The first one has been done for you.

31 = _30_

56 = ___

64 = ___

17 = ___

22 = ___

89 = ___

95 = ___

73 = ___

46 = ___

29 = ___

12 = ___

38 = ___

67 = ___

83 = ___

99 = ___

43 = ___

38 = ___

55 = ___

Round Up Wagon

Skip Counting Practice

Count by 2's. Write in the missing numbers:

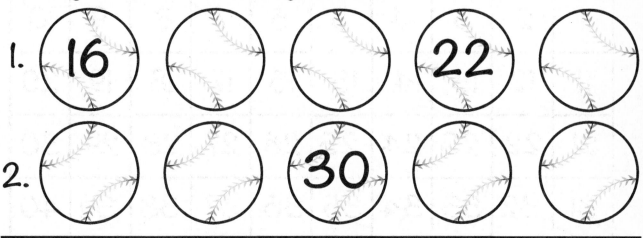

1. 16 ___ ___ 22 ___

2. ___ ___ 30 ___ ___

Count by 5's. Write in the missing numbers:

3. 25 ___ ___ ___ 45

4. ___ 55 ___ ___ ___

Count by 10's. Write in the missing numbers:

5. 10 ___ 30 ___ ___

6. ___ ___ ___ 90 ___

Skip Counting by 2s, 5s and 10s

1. Count by 2s and trace a **red** border around each box that you land on.
2. Then count by 5s and place a **blue** circle around the number in each box that you land on.
3. Finally, count by 10s and place a **green** X over the number in each box that you land on.

1	2	3	4	5	6	7	8	9	10
11	12	13	14	15	16	17	18	19	20
21	22	23	24	25	26	27	28	29	30
31	32	33	34	35	36	37	38	39	40
41	42	43	44	45	46	47	48	49	50
51	52	53	54	55	56	57	58	59	60
61	62	63	64	65	66	67	68	69	70
71	72	73	74	75	76	77	78	79	80
81	82	83	84	85	86	87	88	89	90
91	92	93	94	95	96	97	98	99	100

Challenge

1. If you keep counting on from 100, what is the next number you will trace in **red**?

2. If you keep counting on from 100, what is the next number you will circle in **blue**?

3. If you keep counting on from 100, what is the next number you will X in **green**?

58

Counting to 150

Use this chart to help you count past 100! Fill in the missing numbers starting with 101.

1	2	3	4	5	6	7	8	9	10
11	12	13	14	15	16	17	18	19	20
21	22	23	24	25	26	27	28	29	30
31	32	33	34	35	36	37	38	39	40
41	42	43	44	45	46	47	48	49	50
51	52	53	54	55	56	57	58	59	60
61	62	63	64	65	66	67	68	69	70
71	72	73	74	75	76	77	78	79	80
81	82	83	84	85	86	87	88	89	90
91	92	93	94	95	96	97	98	99	100

Counting on Bananas

Can you help Milo the Monkey find his bunch of bananas?
Connect the even numbers (in order) to show Milo which trees to swing to!

1	2	3	4	5	6	7

8	9	10	11	12	13	14	15	16	17	18

19	20	21	22	23	24	25	26	27	28	29

30	31	32	33	34	35	36	37	38	39	40

41	42	43	44	45	46	47	48	49	50	51

52	53	54	55	56	57	58	59	60	61	62

63	64	65	66	67	68	69	70	71	72	73

74	75	76	77	78	79	80	81	82	83	84

85	86	87	88	89	90	91	92	93	94	95

96	97	98	99	100

A Puppy and a Bone: Odd Numbers

Help Puppy fetch his bone by coloring the spaces with odd numbers to show the path.

Missing Numbers: 1-100

This hundreds chart is missing some numbers. Use your knowledge of number patterns to fill in the chart! You may work in any order you choose! Which pattern is easiest to fill in? You decide!

1	2	★	4	5	6	★	★	9	10
11	★	13	14	★	★	17	18	19	20
21	22	23	★	25	★	27	28	29	★
★	32	33	34	35	36	★	38	★	40
41	42	★	44	★	46	47	★	49	50
51	★	★	54	55	56	57	58	59	★
61	62	63	★	65	★	67	68	★	70
★	72	73	74	75	76	★	★	79	80
★	82	83	★	85	86	87	★	89	90
91	★	93	94	95	★	97	98	★	100

Number Jigsaw: 1-100

Cut this hundreds chart into jigsaw pieces using the colored lines as a guide. Then mix up the pieces and try to put them back together again! Play again with a friend!

1	2	3	4	5	6	7	8	9	10
11	12	13	14	15	16	17	18	19	20
21	22	23	24	25	26	27	28	29	30
31	32	33	34	35	36	37	38	39	40
41	42	43	44	45	46	47	48	49	50
51	52	53	54	55	56	57	58	59	60
61	62	63	64	65	66	67	68	69	70
71	72	73	74	75	76	77	78	79	80
81	82	83	84	85	86	87	88	89	90
91	92	93	94	95	96	97	98	99	100

Hundreds of Pieces!

Use your knowledge of the hundreds chart to fill in the empty boxes on the puzzle pieces below! One of the pieces has been started for you.

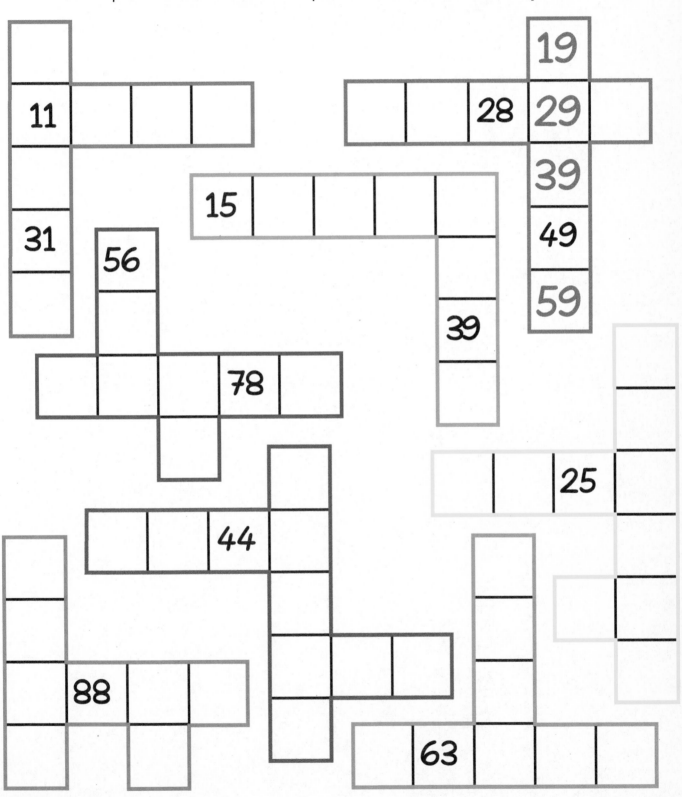

Great job!

_____

is an Education.com math superstar

PATTERNS ON THE GO

Finish the Pattern

Which vehicle comes next? Circle the correct answer.

1.

2.

3.

4.

5.

6.

Finish the Pattern

Which vehicle comes next? Circle the correct answer.

1.

2.

3.

4.

5.

6.

Copy the Colors

Color the vehicle on the right to match the one on the left.
Create your own pattern for the last two vehicles.

Cars on the Road

Which car comes next? Cut out the cars below. Paste them where they belong.

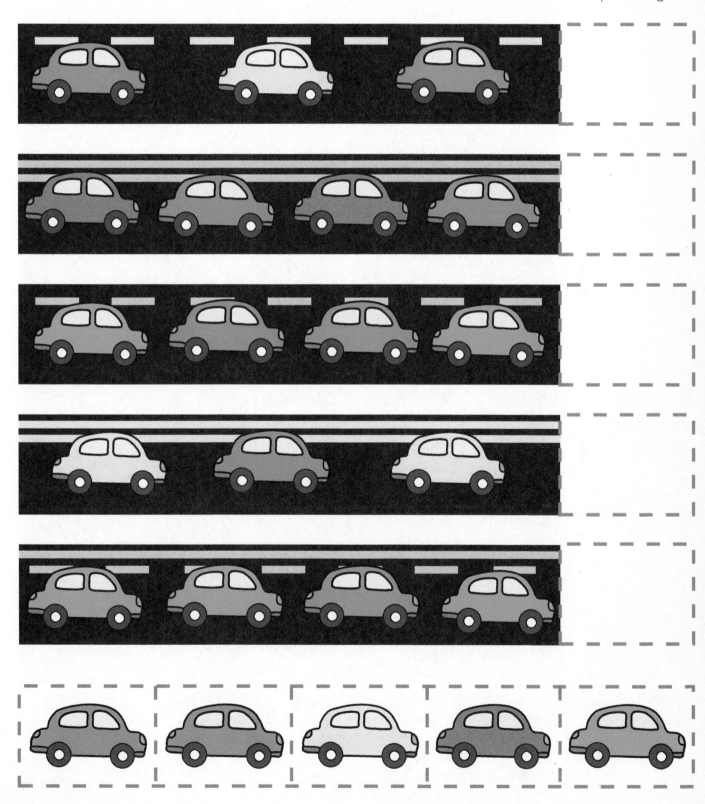

What Kind of Pattern?

Look at the patterns below. Write whether they are ABAB or AABB.

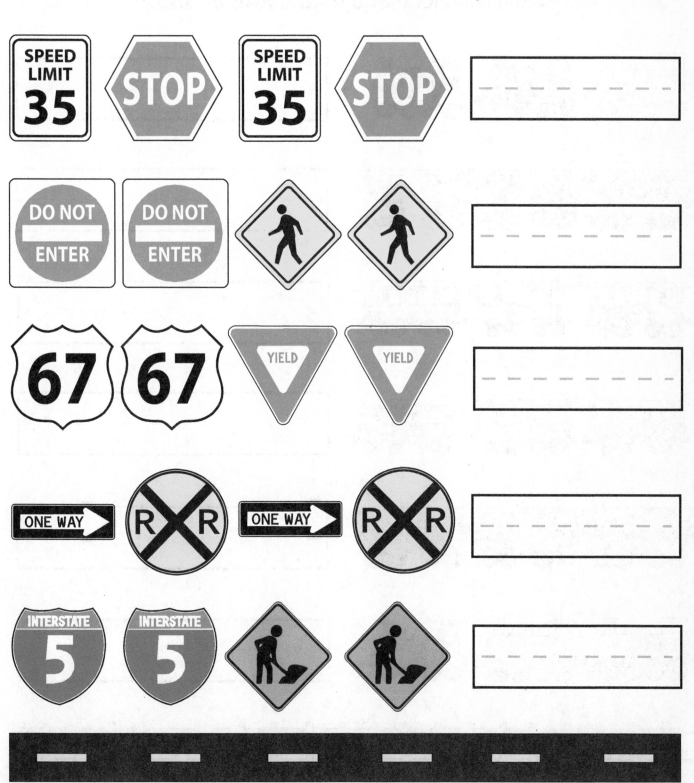

What Kind of Pattern?

Look at the patterns below.
Write whether they are ABA, AAB or ABB.

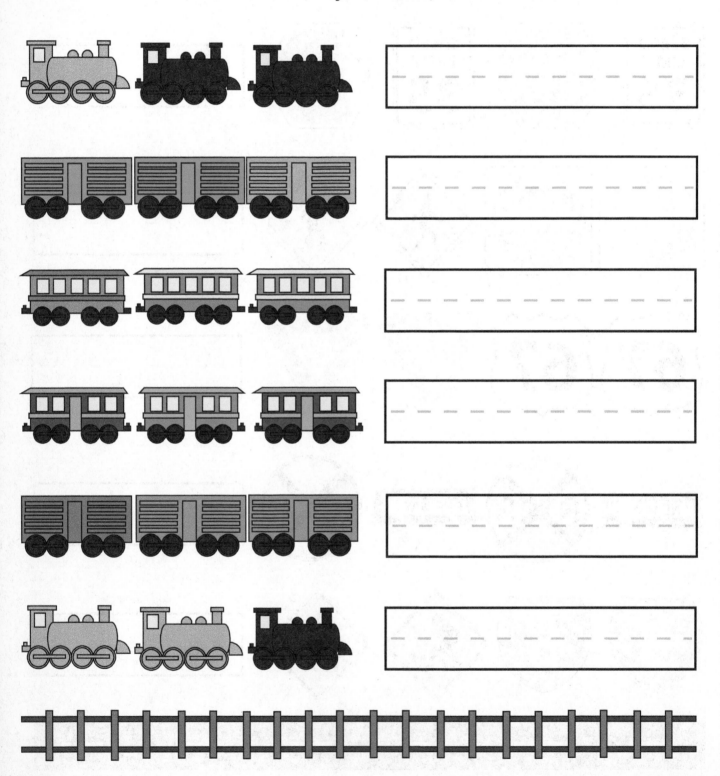

Boats on the Water

Color the last boat on the water to complete the pattern.

Patterns and Traffic Lights

Which traffic light color is missing from each pattern? Circle the correct answer.

1.

2.

3.

4.

5.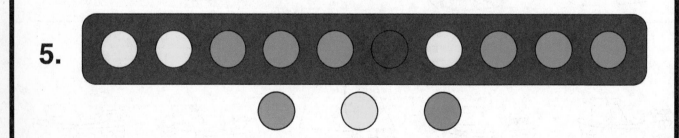

78

Finish the Race

Write the word that would come next in the pattern.

1. slow, fast, slow, fast, slow, fast, slow, fast, _____

2. drive, speed, brake, drive, speed, brake, _____

3. cheer, cheer, clap, clap, cheer, cheer, clap, _____

4. steer, steer, skid, steer, steer, skid, steer, _____

5. track, dash, past, track, dash, past, track, _____

6. first, first, last, last, first, first, last, last, _____

7. flag, prize, prize, flag, prize, prize, flag, _____

8. brag, brag, grand, show, brag, brag, grand, _____

9. glad, crowd, crowd, finish, glad, crowd, crowd, _____

The train is running late!

Help the conductor put the cars in the correct order so that they can leave the station.

Mark the mistake in the pattern with an X. Draw the correct pattern below each train.

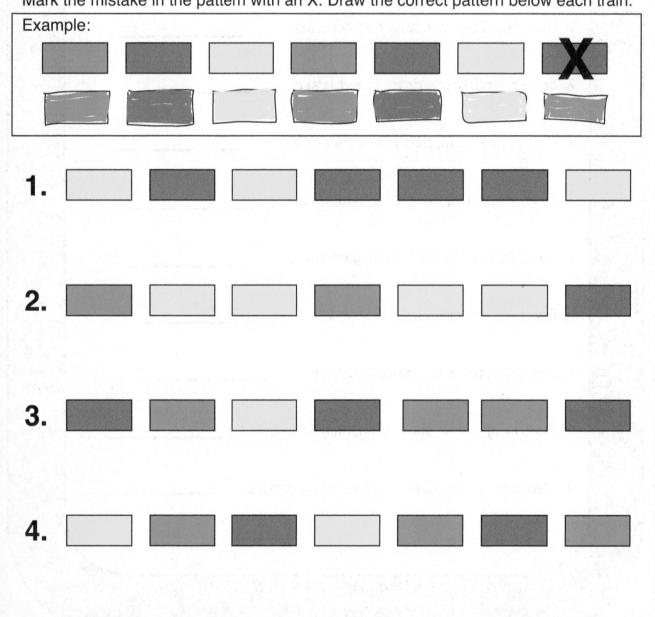

Example:

1.

2.

3.

4.

Traffic Jam

Main Street is super busy! Circle the part that repeats in each pattern.

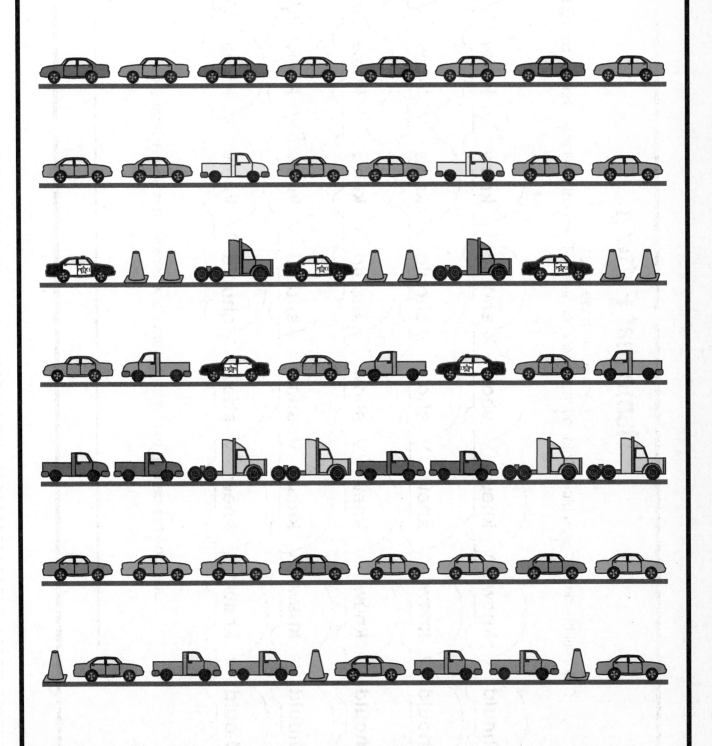

Name that Pattern

Look at all these cars!

Color all the "knew" cars blue. Color all the "show" cars red. Then color all the "should" cars green.

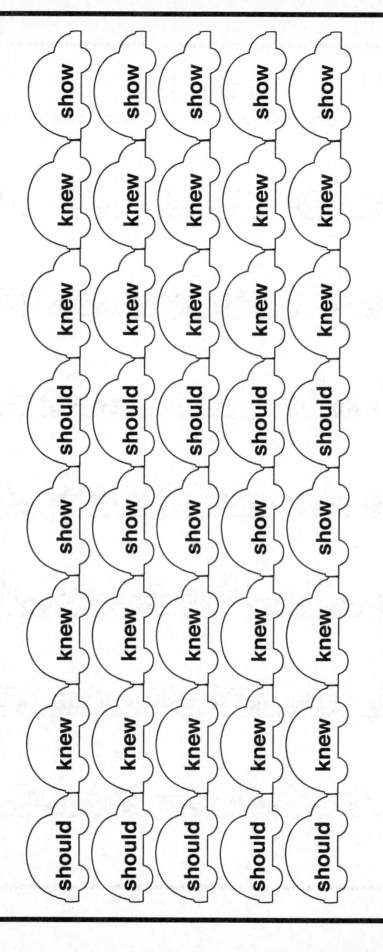

Describe the pattern of this traffic jam (for example: It is an ABC pattern):

_____

82

Name that Pattern

Look at all these cars!

Color all the "again" cars purple. Color all the "your" cars pink. Then color all the "friend" cars yellow.

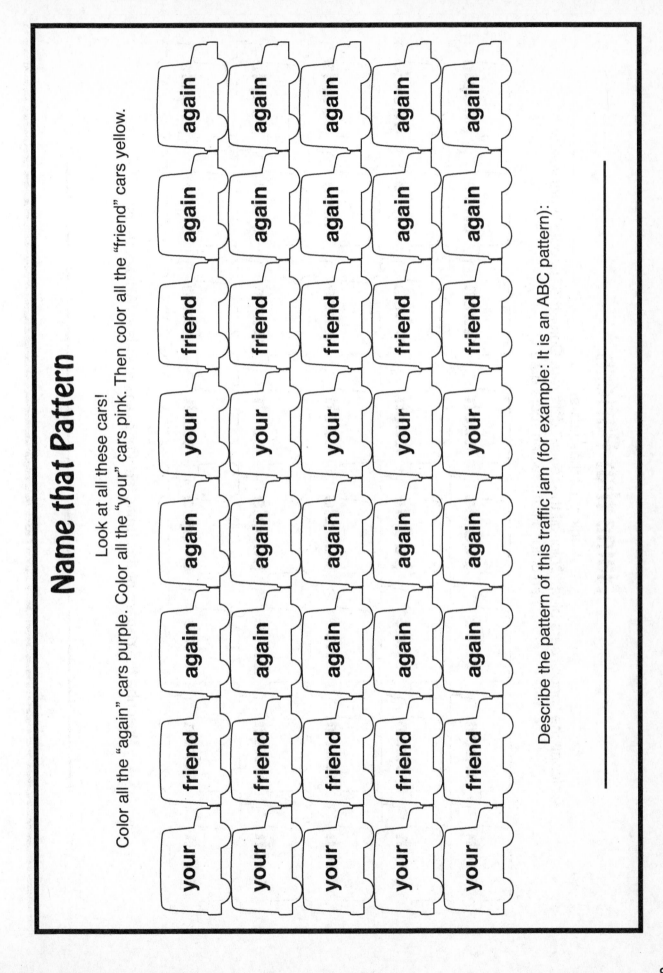

Describe the pattern of this traffic jam (for example: It is an ABC pattern): _____

Name that Pattern

Look at all these cars!

Color all the "once" cars blue. Color all the "each" cars red. Color the "people" cars yellow.
Then color all the "when" cars green.

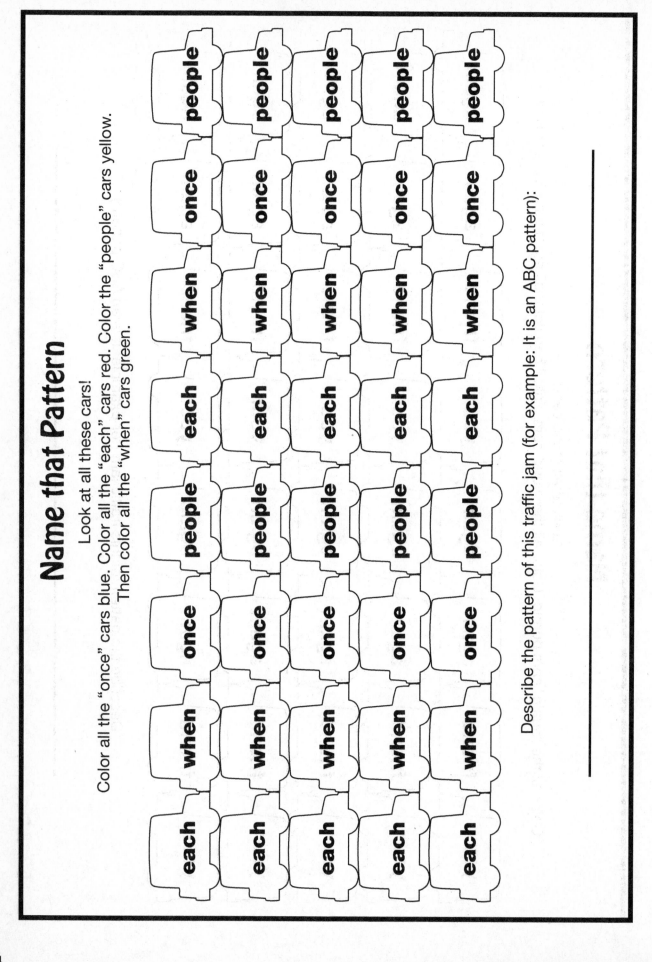

Describe the pattern of this traffic jam (for example: It is an ABC pattern): _____

Patterns on a Hundreds Chart: Rows

When we look at rows, we are looking at the numbers that go across the chart.

Look at each row and find the number that repeats.
Write the number on the line at the end of each row.

1	2	3	4	5	6	7	8	9	10
11	12	13	14	15	16	17	18	19	20
21	22	23	24	25	26	27	28	29	30
31	32	33	34	35	36	37	38	39	40
41	42	43	44	45	46	47	48	49	50
51	52	53	54	55	56	57	58	59	60
61	62	63	64	65	66	67	68	69	70
71	72	73	74	75	76	77	78	79	80
81	82	83	84	85	86	87	88	89	90
91	92	93	94	95	96	97	98	99	100

Patterns on a Hundreds Chart: Rows

1	2	3	4	5	6	7	8	9	10
11	12	13	14	15	16	17	18	19	20
21	22	23	24	25	26	27	28	29	30

Look at the numbers highlighted in yellow.

What do these numbers have in common?

_____

Which number in the second row does not belong? _____

Now look at the numbers highlighted in orange.

What do these numbers have in common?

_____

Which number in the third row does not belong? _____

Patterns on a Hundreds Chart: Columns

When we look at columns, we are looking at the numbers that go down the chart.

Look at each column and find the number that repeats. Write the number on the line underneath the column.

1	2	3	4	5	6	7	8	9	10
11	12	13	14	15	16	17	18	19	20
21	22	23	24	25	26	27	28	29	30
31	32	33	34	35	36	37	38	39	40
41	42	43	44	45	46	47	48	49	50
51	52	53	54	55	56	57	58	59	60
61	62	63	64	65	66	67	68	69	70
71	72	73	74	75	76	77	78	79	80
81	82	83	84	85	86	87	88	89	90
91	92	93	94	95	96	97	98	99	100

___ ___ ___ ___ ___ ___ ___ ___ ___ ___

Driving in All Directions

Find the number in the box on a hundreds chart.
Fill in the number that is above it, below it, and to the left and right of the number.
Tell your grown-up about any patterns that you see.

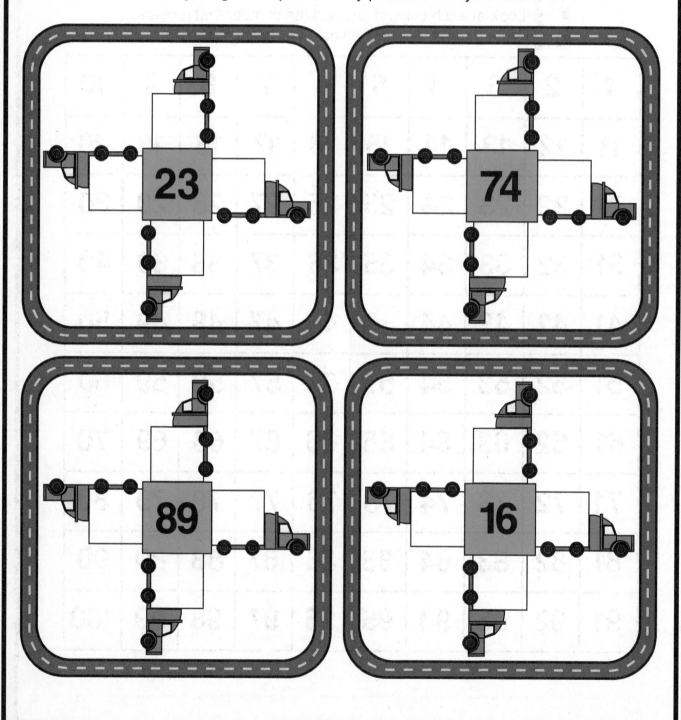

Playing with Patterns

Set Up (2-4 Players):
~ Cut out the cards and pieces. Place the cards face down. Each player gets 4 of each shape.

To Play:
~ Flip over a card. The first player to duplicate the pattern gets the card.
~ Whoever collects the most cards wins!

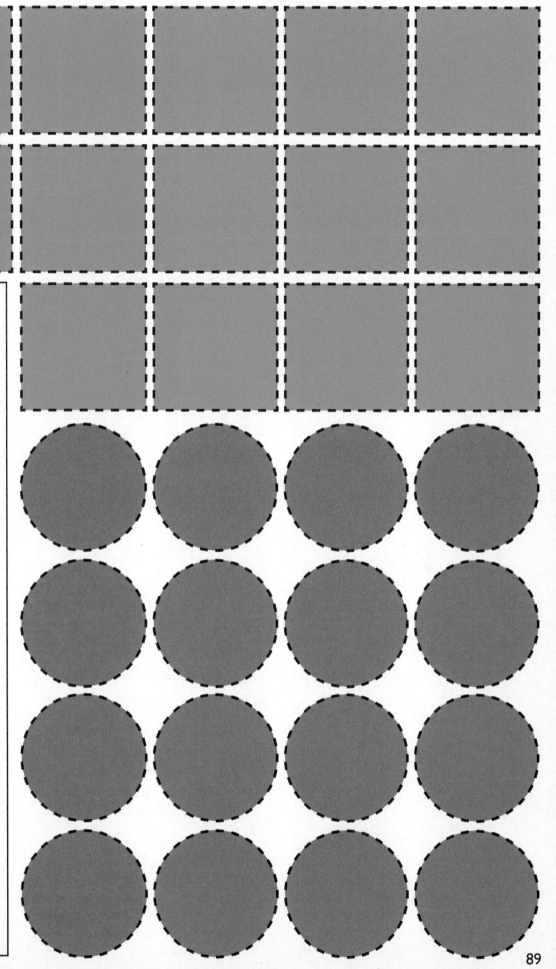

89

Playing with Patterns

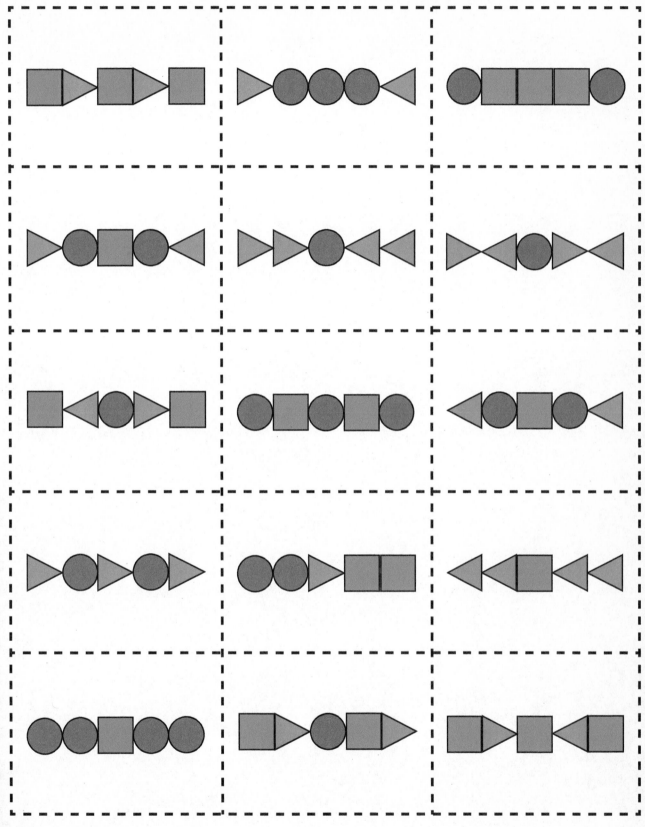

Playing with Patterns

Playing with Patterns

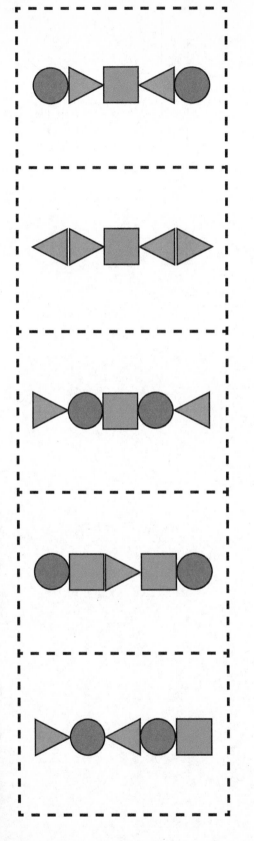

*Extra Challenge

Are you ready for more of a pattern challenge? Then cut out the extra challenge pieces and the rest of the cards!

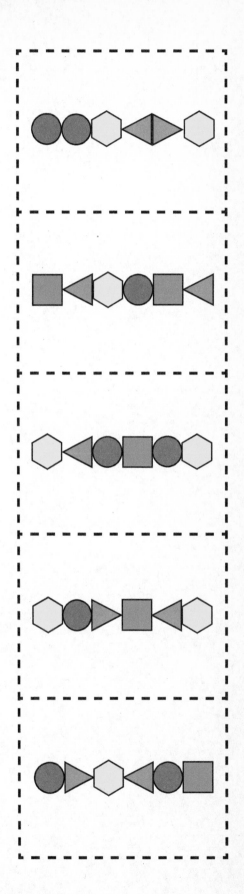

95

Cereal Patterns
by Sue Bradford Edwards

Practice patterning the fun way—by playing with your food! Using cereal and pipe cleaners, help your child create crunchy, edible patterns. Start with a simple ABC pattern and work your way to more complicated patterns as she works on small motor skills and her understanding of patterns. And she can nibble while she works.

What You Need:
- O-shaped cereal in a variety of colors
- Small bowls or cups
- Scissors
- Pipe cleaners
- Masking tape

What You Do:
1. Have your child sort some of the cereal by color, putting each color in a separate bowl or cup. She can also do this on a plate or cutting board.
2. Help her twist two or three pipe cleaners together at the ends to reach just over one foot long. Do this two more times so that she has three foot-long strings.
3. Have her gather groups of cereal pieces in three different colors. Can she lay out an ABC pattern on the table? Get her started threading this pattern onto the string. Encourage her to thread at least six repeats.
4. If necessary, sort more cereal!
5. What other patterns can she make? Ask her to again choose three colors of cereal. Now have her string an AA BB CC on the next string, again stringing several repeats.
6. Now it's your turn! Choose four different cereal pieces. On the table, lay out an A BB CCC DDDD pattern. Ask your child to describe the pattern to you. Now have her string an A BB CCC DDDD pattern of her own.

When you're all done, strung cereal can be hung outside for the birds or unstrung and munched by your young pattern maker.

Nuts and Bolts Sorting Activity
by Gina Dal Fuoco

Does Dad's toolbox need to be tidied up? Get your child to help you clean while sneaking in a little math along the way. Sorting objects by size, color, shape, or function is an important concept in mathematical reasoning, and it's the perfect excuse for a little housekeeping!

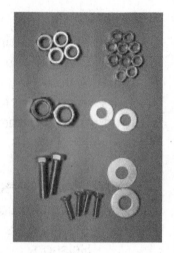

What You Need:
- Various small objects found in a toolbox (screws, nuts, bolts, nails, washers, etc.)
- A sandwich bag

What You Do:
Give your child a sandwich bag full of nuts, bolts, screws, and washers. Tell her that you need her help. Together, you're going to organize these objects and clean up the toolbox or drawer. Now let the sorting begin!

Several key skills make up the nuts and bolts of early math. Here are three ideas for using your actual nuts and bolts (and screws!) to give your child some practice.

Sorting: Give your child the bag and ask her to organize the contents into groups. When she's finished, ask her why she chose to group them in that way. Then challenge her to find another way to group the objects. For example, she might put the screws and nails together because they're all the same length, or the washers and bolts together because they are round. Another way to sort might be screws and nails together because they're silver, and other pieces because they're brass.

Creating Sets: Can your child match up things that work together? Talk to her about the way in which the objects in the toolbox are used. For example, screws and bolts work together as a pair. Ask her to group them. Then ask some questions like "Are there enough of each?" "Which one has more or less?" and "How many more do you need to have equal groups?" This will help your child to see the relationship between the sets, which will serve her well as she begins to move onto more abstract math concepts.

Patterning: When many parents think of patterning practice, they think of beads. But kids can practice patterning with other objects, too! Ask your child to dump out her bag of materials on a table and show her how to create what teachers call an AB pattern. For example, washer, bolt, washer, bolt. Ask your child if she can add to the pattern. What comes next? Once she's comfortable with the AB pattern, challenge her to create her own pattern for *you* to extend. Can she trick you with more and more intricate patterns? Let her try! And be sure to play along. Building patterns teaches children to look for relationships, which will help them later with number combinations.

Math experts agree that young children need many opportunities to practice their math knowledge. Playing "Nuts and Bolts" with your child gives her the opportunity to work on three of them. And you might even get the toolbox or junk drawer cleaned up, too!

Great job!

is an Education.com math superstar

WORD PROBLEMS, NO PROBLEM

Draw & Add

Read the questions below and draw the pictures. Then count your pictures to find the answer.

Billy has 1 pencil and Mark has 4 pencils. How many pencils are there in total?

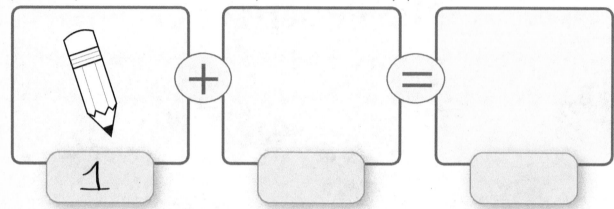

Abi has 2 cars and Jena has 3 cars. How many cars are there in total?

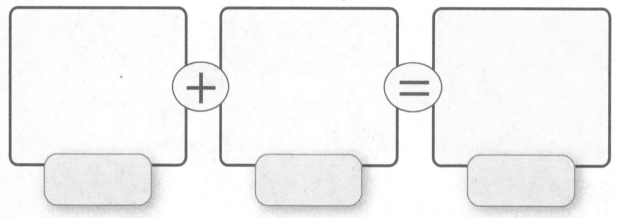

Steve has 5 erasers and Sonia has 3 erasers. How many erasers are there in total?

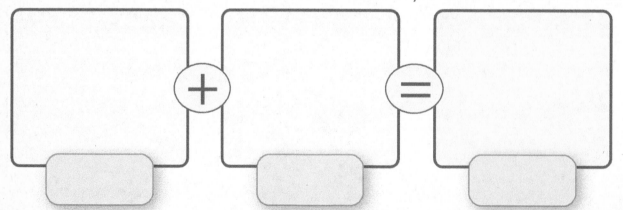

Draw & Add

Read the questions below and draw the pictures. Then count your pictures to find the answer.

Dave has 6 balls and Mike has 3 balls. How many balls are there in total?

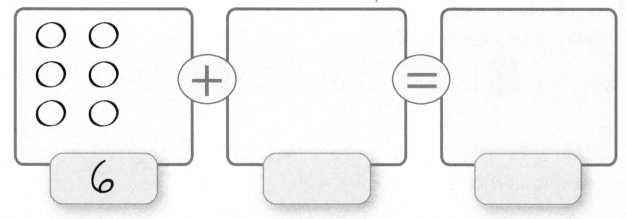

Sunny has 8 dogs and George has 2 dogs. How many dogs are there in total?

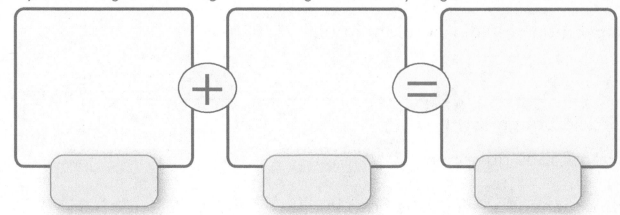

Roy has 7 bats and Tim has 2 bats. How many bats are there in total?

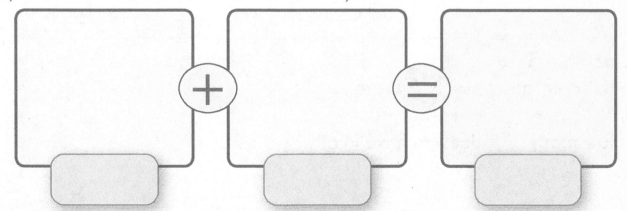

Garden Addition

Read each problem. Write out the number equation and add to find the solution.

Jenna planted 8 .

Amy gave her 5 more .

How many are there in all?

_____ + _____ = _____

Howie planted 6 .

Then he planted 4 more.

 How many did he plant in all?

_____ + _____ = _____

Gracie bought 3 .

Then Robby gave her 7 more.

How many does she have in all?

_____ + _____ = _____

Jack has 9 .

His mom gave him 3 more.

How many 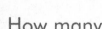 does he have in all?

_____ + _____ = _____

Candy Subtraction Charm

Read each problem. Subtract to find the solution. Write your answer in the space provided.

I bought 11 .
I gave 5 to my brother.

How many do I have now?

You have 8 .
You and your friend ate 3 .

How many do you have now?

I have 10 .
I ate 8 .

How many are left?

You have 12 .
You share 6 with your mom.

How many are there now?

Solve the Story Problems

Read each story problem and solve.

There are 5 apples.
There are 4 grapes.
How many fruits are there in all?

_____fruits

There are 7 bananas.
You buy 2 bananas.
How many bananas are left over?

_____bananas

There were 9 oranges,
but 5 fell to the ground.
How many oranges are left?

_____oranges

There were 3 pears,
but you bought 2 of them.
How many pears are left in the stand?

_____pears

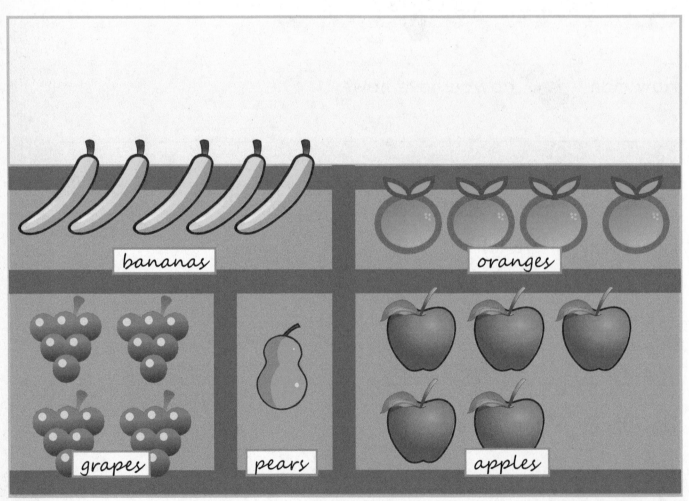

Number Stories Addition

Read the number stories below. Use the orange box next to each problem to show your work. Use pictures, words, and/or numbers to find a solution.

Danny had 5 toy cars. He got 8 more toy cars for his birthday. How many does he have now?

Emily found 4 acorns in the park yesterday. She found another 12 acorns today. How many does she have now?

Jake ate 6 chips at snack. Lisa ate 10 chips at snack. How many chips did the kids eat?

Jill walked 4 blocks to the library yesterday. She also walked 7 blocks to the grocery store. How many blocks did Jill walk?

Robert did 12 sit-ups in PE class. Luke did 9 sit-ups. How many sit-ups did the boys do altogether?

Number Stories Subtraction

Read the number stories below. Use the orange box next to each problem to show your work. Use pictures, words, and/or numbers to find a solution.

Paul had 17 dollars saved up. He spent 6 dollars on a new toy. How much money does he have left?

Anna baked 12 cookies. Her brother ate 6 of them. How many cookies are left?

Nancy has 15 goldfish in her aquarium. Billy has 9 goldfish in his aquarium. How many more goldfish does Nancy have?

Greg had 25 baseball cards. He gave 4 of his cards away to his friend. How many baseball cards does he have left?

Pete collected 36 pieces of Halloween candy. He gave 12 pieces to his brother. How many pieces of candy are left?

Number Jumble

This math homework is mixed up. Can you match each number sentence to the correct picture equation?

6 − 2 = _____

2 + 3 = _____

4 + 2 = _____

5 − 3 = _____

5 + 2 = _____

7 − 5 = _____

Draw & Add

Read the questions below and draw the pictures. Then count your pictures to find the answer.

Kilee has 4 blocks and Tamia has 6 blocks. How many blocks are there in total?

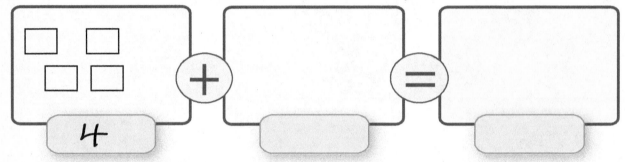

4

Tina has 6 markers and Chuck has 9 markers. How many markers are there in total?

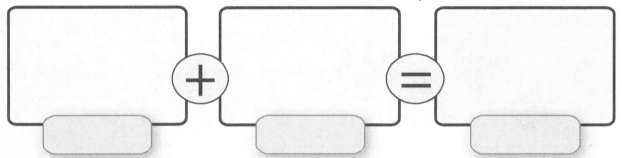

Shane has 2 books and Lisa has 12 books. How many books are there in total?

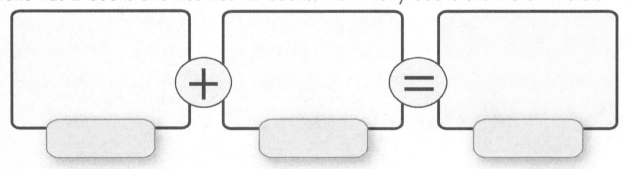

Roy has 11 robots and Remy has 8 robots. How many robots are there in total?

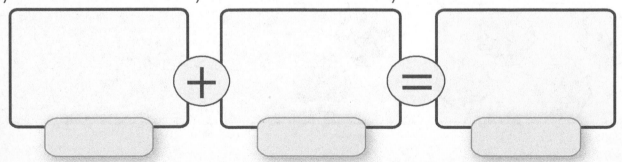

At the Grocery Store

Solve each problem by using the grocery store to fill in the equations.

 5¢  2¢  7¢  3¢  8¢  4¢

Mimi has 10¢. She bought a banana and a pear. How much does she have left?

_____ + _____ = _____ and 10 − _____ = _____

Trudy bought 1 carrot and an apple. How much did she spend?

_____ + _____ = _____

Thomas has 8¢. He bought a banana. How much does he have left?

_____ − _____ = _____

Cory bought an orange and celery. How much did he spend?

_____ + _____ = _____

Ben has 12¢. He bought an apple. How much does he have left?

_____ − _____ = _____

At the Art Store

Solve each problem by using the store to fill in the equations.

3¢   5¢   7¢   6¢   2¢   9¢

Tia bought 3 markers. How much did she spend?

_____ + _____ + _____ = _____

Sharon has 20¢. She bought 1 paintbrush and 1 pen. How much does she have left?

_____ + _____ = _____ and 20 − _____ = _____

Frankie bought 2 paint tubes. How much did he spend?

_____ + _____ = _____

Rocky has 17¢. He bought 4 pencils. How much does he have left?

_____ + _____ + _____ + _____ = _____ and 17 − _____ = _____

Rachel bought 1 marker and 1 tube of paint. How much did she spend?

_____ + _____ = _____

Draw & Add

Read the questions below and draw the pictures. Then count your pictures to find the answer.

Amy has 3 stars and Ann has 8 stars. How many stars are there in total?

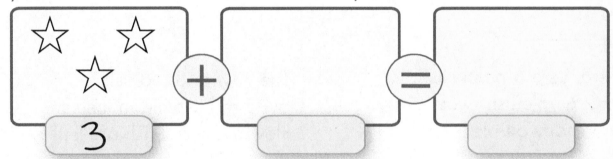

Paul has 7 bricks and Dan has 6 bricks. How many bricks are there in total?

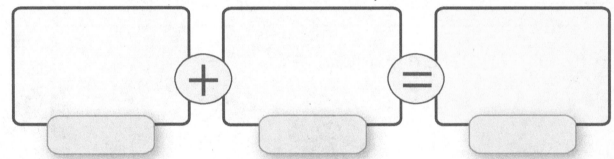

Mia has 5 jacks and Suzy has 9 jacks. How many jacks are there in total?

Mike has 3 cards and Lily has 10 cards. How many cards are there in total?

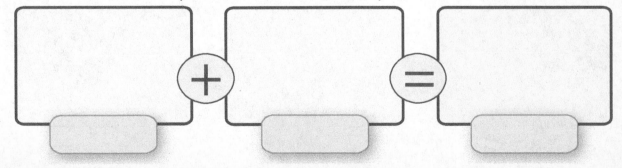

Solve the Story Problems

Read each story problem and solve.

There are 3 blue fish.
There are 3 green fish.
How many fish are there in all?

_____fish

There are 2 orange fish.
4 yellow fish join them.
How many fish are there in all?

_____fish

There were 6 purple fish,
but 2 purple fish swam away.
How many purple fish are left ?

_____purple fish

There were 8 red fish,
but 5 red fish hid in the sand.
How many red fish are left?

_____red fish

At School

Read each problem. Use the picture graph to help you answer the questions.

Ben has 3 pencils, 5 crayons and 1 eraser. How many does he have in all?

_____ supplies

Jenny has 2 markers, 3 pens and 6 paintbrushes. How many does she have in all?

_____ supplies

Robbie has 3 erasers, 4 markers and 5 colored pencils. How many does he have in all?

_____ supplies

Tina has 4 scissors, 5 sharpeners and 3 pencils. How many does she have in all?

_____ supplies

Mimi's Fabulous Music Shop

There's a sale going on at Mimi's Fabulous Music Shop!
Use addition or subtraction to solve the word problems.
Show your work.

Mrs. Jensen bought 5 tambourines, 2 kazoos, and 4 recorder flutes for her class. How many instruments did Mrs. Jensen buy in all?

_____ instruments

There are 20 guitar picks in a sale bin. At the end of the day there are only 5 left. How many were sold?

_____ guitar picks

Jackson the drummer needs new sticks! He spends $2 on regular drum sticks, $5 on a mallet, and $10 on brushes. How much money does he spend in all?

$ _____

9 people came into the store. The first person bought 12 guitar strings and left. 3 more people left after they each bought a tuner. How many people are left? How many items were bought?

CHALLENGE

_____ items

Fresh Fruit Salad Anyone?

Directions: Use addition to solve the word problems below.

Tommy made a fruit salad for the neighborhood block party. He put 5 grapes in a bowl. He added 6 pieces of watermelon and 3 strawberries. Finally, Tommy added 4 slices of banana.

How many pieces of fruit did Tommy use to make his fruit salad for the party?

_____

Jane made a different version of fruit salad for the party. She used 12 melon balls and 8 slices of orange. She also put 14 blueberries into the bowl before mixing it all up.

How many pieces of fruit did Jane use altogether?

_____

Kim's mom had also prepared a fruit salad for the party. She put in lots and lots of raspberries because Kim LOVES raspberries. There were already 16 raspberries in the salad but Kim wanted more so she added 9 more.

How many raspberries did Kim end up with in her mom's fruit salad?

_____

If you were going to this party and had to bring your own fruit salad, what would you mix together? Choose at least 3 different types of fruit and create your own fruit salad word problem in the space below!

_____

_____

How Does Your Garden Grow?

Read each number story below. You will need to either add or subtract to find the answer. Use the empty space to show your work using pictures, words or numbers.

Susie planted 5 tulips, 7 daisies, and 4 roses in her garden. How many flowers did she plant altogether?

_____

Tim picked 3 whole watermelons and 15 strawberries from his garden on Sunday. How many pieces of fruit did Tim pick altogether?

_____

Larry planted 25 green peppers in his garden but only 17 of them were ripe enough to pick. How many green peppers were left in the garden?

_____

On Thursday, Kate picked 12 tomatoes and 9 cucumbers from her garden. On Saturday, she picked 7 more tomatoes and 3 more cucumbers.

How many tomatoes did Kate pick altogether?   _____
How many cucumbers did Kate pick altogether?   _____
Which vegetable did Kate pick more of?
How many more?   _____

Challenge:
On which day did Kate pick fewer vegetables?   _____
How many fewer vegetables did she pick that day? _____

Word Problem Challenge

Write an addition or subtraction sentence for each word problem.
Solve the problem.

Farmer Green gathered 36 eggs from his chickens. His wife used 8 of them to make breakfast. How many eggs did Farmer Green have left?

_____

There are 42 sheep grazing in Farmer Green's pasture. Each sheep has 1 lamb. How many sheep and lambs are in the pasture in all?

_____

Farmer Green needs 100 apple trees for his orchard. He has 53 apple trees now. How many apple trees does he need to buy?

_____

Mrs. Green brought 75 jars of home-made jam to the farmer's market. She sold 49 jars. How many jars did she have left?

_____

Farmer Green has 22 brown cows, 16 black cows, and 4 tan cows. How many cows does he have in all?

_____

Farmer Green planted 18 rows of corn before lunch. He planted 31 more rows after lunch. How many rows of corn did he plant that day?

_____